VEGGIES
from the Good Earth
APPLIQUÉ ALBUM

BEA OGLESBY

Located in Paducah, Kentucky, the American Quilter's Society (AQS) is dedicated to promoting the accomplishments of today's quilters. Through its publications and events, AQS strives to honor today's quiltmakers and their work and to inspire future creativity and innovation in quiltmaking.

EDITOR: SHELLEY HAWKINS
GRAPHIC DESIGN: AMY CHASE
COVER DESIGN: MICHAEL BUCKINGHAM
PHOTOGRAPHY: CHARLES R. LYNCH

Library of Congress Cataloging-in-Publication Data
Oglesby, Bea, 1924–
   Veggies from the good earth : appliqué album / by Bea Oglesby.
       p. cm.
   Summary: "Fifteen vegetable patterns to make together in one quilt or singly or grouped for pillows, table runners, wallhangings, etc. Includes instructions and tips for choosing colors. Use with any appliqué technique. Color illustrations and full-sized patterns provided for three projects"– Provided by pubisher.
   ISBN 1-57432-921-9
1. Appliqué–Patterns. 2. Vegetables in art. I. Title.

TT779.0347 2006
746.44'5041–dc22

                            2006023928

Additional copies of this book may be ordered from the American Quilter's Society, PO Box 3290, Paducah, KY 42002-3290; 800-626-5420 (orders only please); or online at www.AmericanQuilter.com. For all other inquiries, please call 270-898-7903.

Definitions of vegetables are adapted from the *Merriam Webster Online Dictonary* [http://www.m-w.com], based on the print version of *Merriam-Webster's Collegiate® Dictionary, Eleventh Edition.*

Dedication

To my daughters, Corinne, Janet, and Elise, who have been my most faithful cheerleaders.

To my husband, Red, for his encouragement, his cooperation, his patience, his physical and mental support, and most of all, his good humor.

Acknowledgments

These vegetables have been a joy to work on and I wish to thank the many people who helped with input, advice, and support.

To my husband and three daughters who "taste-tested" these veggies and advised me as to which patterns should be included and which should not.

To my friends at my local quilt shops: Carol Kirchhoff at Prairie Point, Debbie Richards at Quilter's Haven, and Elaine Johnson at Harper's Fabric and Quilt Company. I thank you all for your patience and guidance in helping me find the perfect fabric for all of these veggies.

To the many students who have taken my classes. Because of their enthusiasm and eagerness, I have been inspired to be a better teacher.

To Barbara Smith, Shelley Hawkins, and all the special people at American Quilter's Society for their belief in me and for the opportunity to make this book a reality.

Contents

Preface

Vegetables are a most important key to our good health and well being. This is not a book on nutrition, but I do share with you some of the most common vegetables that I especially enjoy.

As a child, we heard the familiar words from our parents to clean our plates. We were told that the spinach would make us strong and the carrots would help our eyes. It was not explained to us and we didn't understand it, but now we hear from doctors and dietitians to eat five a day and children's television programs emphasize the importance of veggies and their nutrition.

A vegetable is basically any part of a plant that can be eaten. This can consist of the flower and bud, such as the artichoke; the leaves, such as lettuce, cabbage, and all sorts of greens; the stems, such as broccoli; the pods, such as green beans and peas; and the root vegetables, such as potatoes, beets, and carrots.

The more that scientists study the vegetables we eat, the more evidence is found that they are essential to preventing disease and maintaining good health. An assortment of vegetables can supply

us with all our needed vitamins. They also supply the most reliable source of carbohydrates that give our bodies energy and fuel.

In the United States, we eat a smaller range of vegetables than in many other countries, but with imports from neighboring countries, we are now introduced to many new vegetables, giving us an assortment year round. It is interesting to explore some of these unusual veggies and use them in our meals.

City life and today's fast pace do not often allow room or time for a garden. However, many of us do have a small spot off the kitchen to plant a few tomatoes, peppers, parsley, and basil (a salad right there), or we can grow these in terra-cotta pots on the patio. We can fill a bowl with freshly picked tomatoes or assorted peppers and have a delightful centerpiece for our table. There are also many farmers' markets open on weekends throughout the spring, summer, and fall where fresh veggies are available.

With all the vegetables available to us year round, one does not have to be a vegetarian to enjoy this good earth's bounty.

Introduction

The 15 vegetable patterns (pages 11–55) can be used as a single design, or 12 can be used as a quilt with the green bean border (page 56) or a plain border if desired. The basket filled with veggies (page 66) can be a small wallhanging, or it can be used in the center of a larger wallhanging surrounded by 12 veggies. Four veggie blocks can make another small wallhanging, or a table runner of three blocks can be made. Choose your favorite veggies to use as you desire.

Technically, only 14 of the patterns are considered vegetables because the botanical classification of the tomato is a fruit. However, the tomato is eaten and used as a vegetable, and I cannot imagine making a vegetable quilt without it.

The patterns in Veggies from the Good Earth (page 56) are appliquéd on 13" finished squares. Each veggie pattern can fit on an 11" or larger block. The vegetable blocks, green bean border, and the large Veggie Wallhanging (page 76) were all appliquéd by hand using the freezer-paper method.

The pieces in the vegetable patterns range from 16 for the broccoli to 77 for the artichokes. Instructions and tips for the appliqué and colors are given for each pattern. There are 106 pieces in the large Veggies in a Basket wallhanging, but by appliquéing each vegetable in turn, it was not difficult. The small Veggie Wallhanging was appliquéd with fusible web and edged with machine stitching.

Fabric amounts for the different projects are included, but the amount of fabric needed for your project will depend on what you plan to make. Feel free to change my color selections to blend with your background fabric of choice.

Veggie Essentials

Fabric Selection

Because there are so many colors in these quilts, it is best to choose all or most of your fabrics before cutting. Sometimes a 4" square is all that is needed, but it is good to have an overall view of the colors to ensure that they blend with each other and your background.

If your background is light or white, you may want purple onions, but if your background is dark, white onions would work better. This is not to say that you must use your original choice. Like most projects, changes can and will be made as you work.

On the whole, fabric selection for the veggies should not be a problem because carrots are orange and broccoli is green, but you will need some assorted shades in these colors. Care must be taken in the fabric choices of the leaves and stems. You will need a minimum of 12 different green fabrics, both light and dark, that will blend together and still be distinct from one another.

Fabric Preparation

1. To prepare fabrics, wash with detergent and rinse well. This will remove sizing and any color bleeding that may occur.

2. Keeping the grain straight, cut the blocks the required size. As you cut, mark the top of each block with a "T." This guarantees that the grain lines of the blocks will be the same throughout the quilt.

3. Spray the background fabric with a light application of starch, and iron before marking the pattern. This gives the background a smooth finish and makes it easier to mark.

Appliqué Preparation

1. Center the pattern under the background fabric and hold it in place with masking tape. Use a washout marker or a hard-lead mechanical pencil and trace the entire pattern on the background fabric.

2. On the dull side of freezer paper, trace each piece of the veggie block and number the pieces as indicated. This is the appliqué sequence. Cut out each piece on the drawn line.

3. Iron the pieces individually on the right side of the desired fabrics. For the stitching line, trace each piece with a washout marker. Cut around the pieces leaving a ¼" allowance. As you appliqué, this allowance can be trimmed closer, if needed, for a neat turn-under.

Appliquéing

1. Appliqué each pattern in its numbered sequence. Beginning with piece #1, with the freezer paper in place, turn the seam allowance to the back and crease the seam line with your thumbnail and finger.

2. Remove the freezer paper and position the piece on the marked pattern of your background block. This can be held in place with one or two pins if the appliqué piece is large.

3. Your thread choice should match the appliqué piece. With 100% cotton thread, the finer the better, blind stitch the piece in place keeping stitches ⅛" apart. Continue in this manner until all the pieces are appliquéd.

Artichokes

ar·ti·choke 1 : a tall Mediterranean composite herb *(Cynara scolymus)* resembling a thistle with coarse pinnately incised leaves; also : its edible immature flower head which is cooked as a vegetable

77 Pieces

Do not let the number of pieces scare you. This is not a difficult pattern to appliqué.

Color

Only two fabrics were used in this pattern. One was a mottled green for the stalks and leaves. The petals of the globe artichoke were appliquéd with one green-and-violet batik fabric. By fussy cutting the individual pieces, it was not difficult to distinguish between the petals, having the pink and violet shades at the top and the green shades near the stems. When appliquéing the artichokes, work with one at a time and complete it before you start the next one. In this way, you are able to critique your color choices.

Appliqué Tips

Leave a small section of stalk 3 open where leaf 53 attaches. After leaf 53 is appliquéd, sew down this section of stalk 3.

Finishing

The veins on the leaves can be quilted during the final quilting of the pattern.

For needle-turn appliqué, add a ¼" turn-
under allowance, then trim closer when
appliquéing.

Beets

beet : a biennial garden plant (*Beta vulgaris*) of the goosefoot family that includes several cultivars (as Swiss chard and sugar beet) and that has thick edible leaves with long petioles and often swollen purplish-red roots; also : its root used especially as a vegetable, as a source of sugar, or for forage

21 Pieces

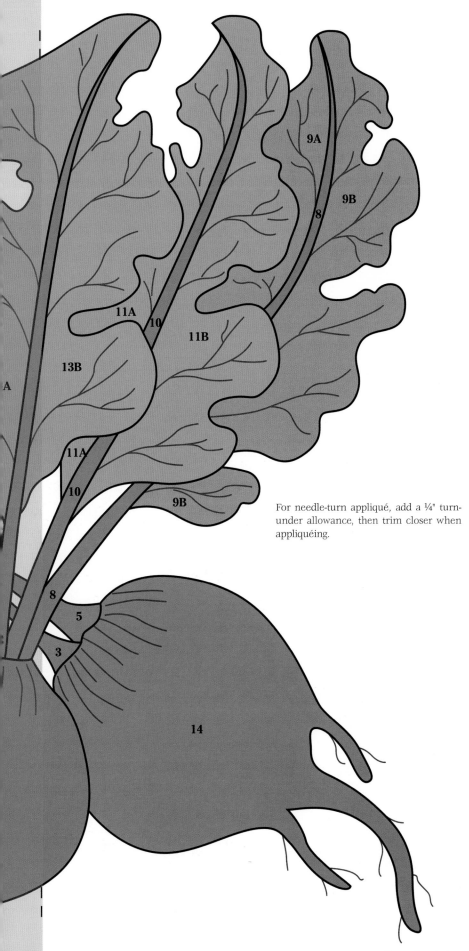

For needle-turn appliqué, add a ¼" turn-under allowance, then trim closer when appliquéing.

Color

This pattern contains four different green fabrics for the leaves, two reddish purple fabrics for the beets and stems, and pink for 16, 18, and 20. The fabric in the leaf veins is the same fabric in the beets. Plan to place the darker fabrics in the back with the lighter fabrics in the front when choosing leaf fabrics.

Appliqué Tips

To get a very narrow vein in the leaves, appliqué the lower section of the leaf stem in place with the seam allowance turned under. Baste the vein fabric that is under the leaf onto the background. Cut the leaf patterns, 4, 6, 9, 11, and 13, in half on the vein line and label them A and B. Treat these leaves as two pieces. Appliqué A first, then B. In this way, a narrow vein can be achieved. On the tips of the leaves, whip part B over part A with tiny stitches.

Finishing

The veins on the leaves can be quilted during the final quilting of the pattern.

6B

6A

4B

3

4A

5

3

2

1

1

13A

13

20

18   16

19

17

7   12

8

3

21

15

For needle-turn appliqué, add a ¼" turn-
under allowance, then trim closer when
appliquéing.

Broccoli

broc·co·li : either of two garden vegetable plants closely related to the cabbage: (1) : one with a thick central stem and a compact head of dense usually green florets that is classified with the cauliflower (2) : one *(Brassica oleracea italica)* with slender stems and usually green or purple florets not arranged in a central head

16 Pieces

2B

2A

1

12

19

13

14

16

4B

3

4A

9

11

10

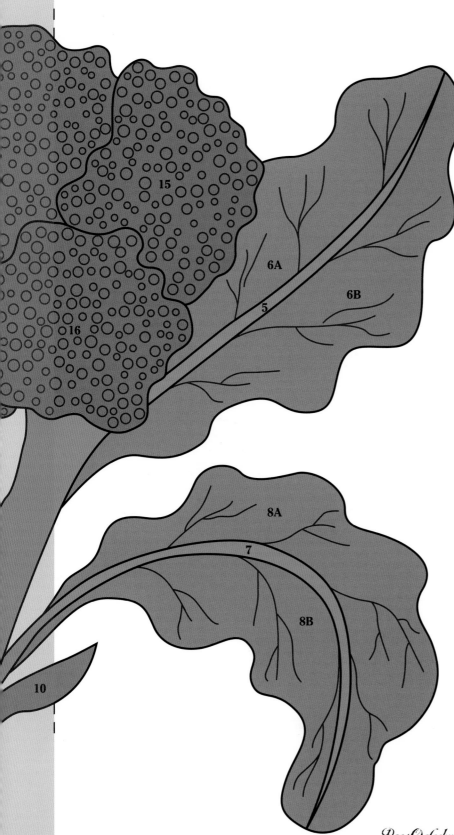

Color

Five or six green fabrics were used in this pattern. Because green is the only color, we must be able to distinguish between the veins, leaves, stems, and broccoli florets.

Appliqué Tips

To get very narrow veins in the four leaves, appliqué the lower section of the vein in place. Baste the vein fabric that is under the leaf onto the background. Cut the leaf patterns in half and label them A and B. Treat each leaf as two pieces and appliqué in place. Whip B over A with tiny stitches.

Finishing

The veins on the leaves can be quilted during the final quilting of the pattern.

For needle-turn appliqué, add a ¼" turn-under allowance, then trim closer when appliquéing.

Carrots

car·rot 1 : a biennial herb (*Daucus carota* of the family *Umbelliferae*, the carrot family) with a usually orange spindle-shaped edible root; also : its root

19 Pieces

Color

This pattern consists of three different medium shades of green fabric for the leaf stems and two different shades of orange for the carrots.

Finishing

To achieve the lacy look of carrot leaves, embroider the leaves with three strands of floss and a stem stitch. Start the embroidery right at the tips of the stems and match the floss to the color of the stem fabric.

For needle-turn appliqué, add a ¼" turn-under allowance, then trim closer when appliquéing.

For needle-turn appliqué, add a ¼" turn-under allowance, then trim closer when appliquéing.

Cauliflower

cau·li·flow·er : a garden plant *(Brassica oleracea botrytis)* related to the cabbage and grown for its compact edible head of usually white undeveloped flowers; also : its flower cluster used as a vegetable

23 Pieces

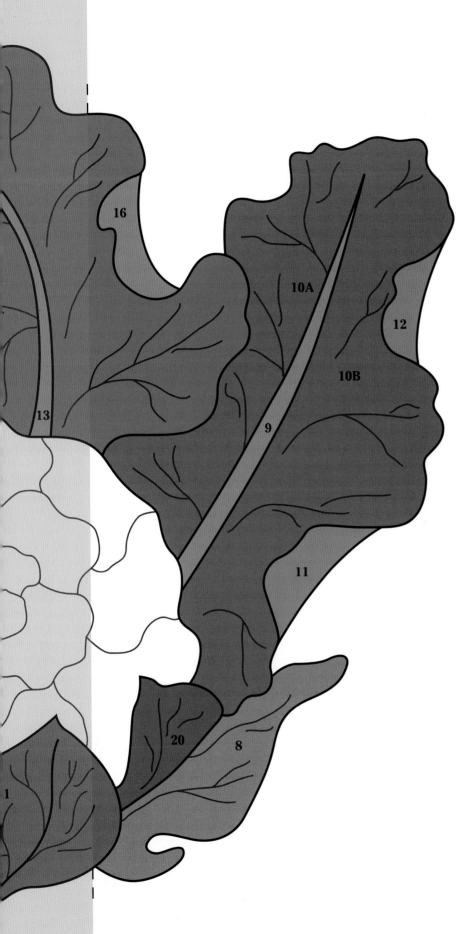

Color

One white fabric was used for the cauliflower. If the background shadows through the white fabric, it is wise to line the cauliflower, which will give you a much sharper image. To line, cut a piece of white muslin the exact size of the cauliflower pattern and baste it onto the background fabric. Appliqué the cauliflower fabric over the lining. A light green was used for the veins in the leaves and the leaf turnover. Several shades of deeper green were used for the leaves.

Appliqué Tips

To get the very narrow veins in the leaves, use the same technique that was used for the beets (page 15).

Finishing

Small veins in the leaves and cauliflower florets can be quilted during the final quilting of the pattern.

For needle-turn appliqué, add a ¼" turn-under allowance, then trim closer when appliquéing.

Corn

corn : 1 : a small hard seed 2 a : the seeds of a cereal grass and especially of the important cereal crop of a particular region (as wheat in Britain, oats in Scotland and Ireland, and Indian corn in the New World and Australia) b : the kernels of sweet corn served as a vegetable while still soft and milky

25 Pieces

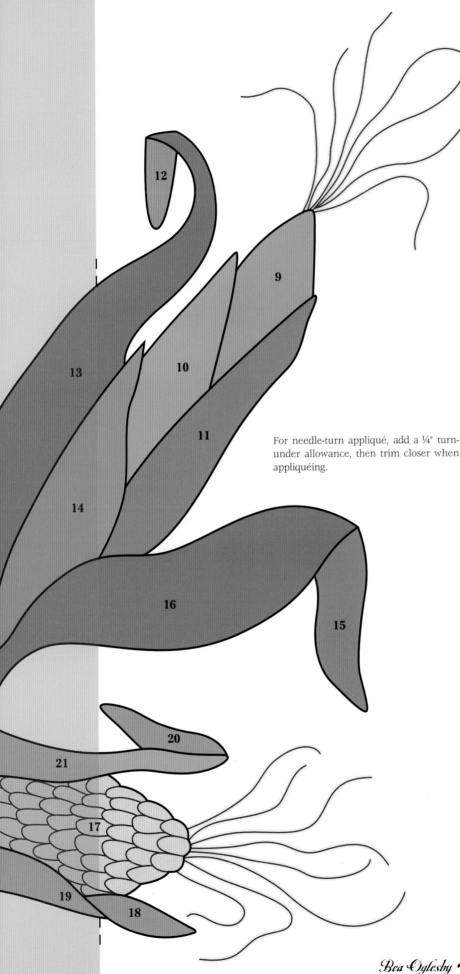

For needle-turn appliqué, add a ¼" turn-under allowance, then trim closer when appliquéing.

Color

Four different green fabrics were used for the corn husks, two shades of brown for 24 and 25, and six different shades of gold for the corn.

Appliqué Tips

For each ear of corn, cut two strips of fabric ¾" x 12" of six gold fabrics. Sew these 12 strips together, alternating the fabrics with a scant ¼" seam allowance. Press flat with all the seam allowances open for less bulk on the back of the pieced strips. From the pieced strips, cut ¾" wide strips perpendicular to the seams. Sew these strips back together, offsetting colors to create the look of corn kernels. You do not have to be accurate in sewing these strips together. Corn kernels are different sizes. Press seam allowances open and flat with a steam iron. Place pattern pieces 1 and 17 on your newly made fabric, mark, cut out with a seam allowance, and appliqué.

Finishing

For the corn silk, embroider with two strands of yellow or gold floss using the stem stitch.

For needle-turn appliqué, add a ¼" turn-under allowance, then trim closer when appliquéing.

Eggplant

egg·plant : 1 a : a widely cultivated perennial Asian herb (*Solanum melongena*) of the nightshade family yielding edible fruit b : the usually smooth ovoid typically blackish-purple or white fruit of the eggplant

27 Pieces

Color

Hand-dyed lavender was used for the flowers – two or three shades of lavender would work as well. There are many shades of eggplant. Use any color you desire, but choose two different fabrics to distinguish one eggplant from another. Use three different green fabrics in the leaves for variety.

Appliqué Tips

Leave a small section of 17 open until 22 is appliquéd, then complete 17. Leave a small section of 22 open until 27 is appliquéd, then complete 22.

Finishing

Embroider the stamens in the flowers with black floss. The veins can be quilted during the final quilting of the pattern.

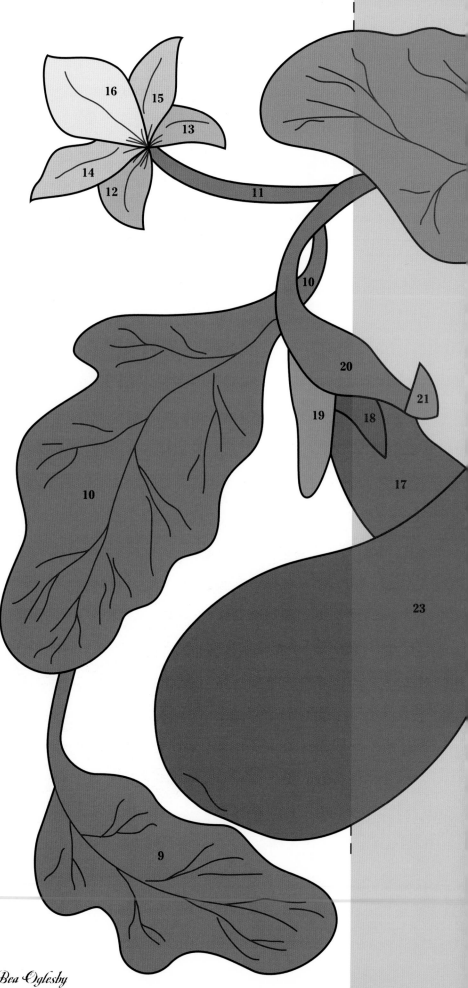

For needle-turn appliqué, add a ¼" turn-under allowance, then trim closer when appliquéing.

Green Beans

green·bean : 1 a : BROAD BEAN b : the seed of any of various erect or climbing plants (as of the genera *Phaseolus* and *Vigna*) of the legume family other than the broad bean c : a plant bearing beans d : an immature bean pod used as a vegetable

26 Pieces

Color

Two shades of lavender were used for the flowers. The beans can be several colors – green, yellow-green, yellow, or beige. Two different shades of green were used for the leaves and bean vine.

Appliqué Tips

Leave an opening in vine 24 to insert the stem of green bean 26. The easiest way to appliqué twisted vines 12 and 13 is to work on them both at the same time. Work one section of 12, then a section of 13, running your needle from one vine to another until you work down to the leaf and flower.

Finishing

The leaf veins can be quilted during the final quilting of the pattern.

For needle-turn appliqué, add a ¼" turn-under allowance, then trim closer when appliquéing.

For needle-turn appliqué, add a ¼" turn-under allowance, then trim closer when appliquéing.

Kohlrabi

kohl·ra·bi : a cabbage (*Brassica oleracea gongylodes*) having a greatly enlarged, fleshy, turnip-shaped edible stem; also : its stem used as a vegetable

38 Pieces

Color

For the kohlrabi, use a very pale green, off-white, or greenish yellow fabric. Use a deeper shade of the kohl-rabi fabric for the stems. Use two or three shades of deep green for the leaves so that each leaf will be distinct.

Appliqué Tips

For a very narrow vein in the leaves, appliqué and baste the vein fabric onto the background in the same manner as the beets (page 15).

Finishing

The veins in the leaves can be quilted during the final quilting of the pattern.

For needle-turn appliqué, add a ¼" turn-under allowance, then trim closer when appliquéing.

Okra

o·kra : a tall annual herb (*Abelmoschus esculentus*) of the mallow family that is cultivated for its mucilaginous green pods used especially in soups or stews; also : the pods of this plant

39 Pieces

My daughter, who dislikes okra in any form, told me I ruined my veggie quilt by including this vegetable. The plant belongs to the mallow family, has a lovely flower similar to the hibiscus, and has an edible pod that is used in gumbos, soups, and stews. It is also delicious deep fried and is a wonderful, versatile vegetable.

Color

Three shades of yellow were used to distinguish between the flower petals. Five different green fabrics were used for the pods, leaves, and stem.

Appliqué Tips

Baste the seed pieces, 26, 34, 36, and 38, onto the background fabric, then appliqué the pod shell pieces over them. The stems of the pods, 29, 30, and 32, should be brown.

Finishing

The veins in the pods and leaves can be quilted during the final quilting of the pattern.

For needle-turn appliqué, add a ¼" turn-under allowance, then trim closer when appliquéing.

Veggie Patterns - Okra

For needle-turn appliqué, add a ¼" turn-under allowance, then trim closer when appliquéing.

Onions

on·ion 1 : a widely cultivated Asian herb (*Allium cepa*) of the lily family with pungent edible bulbs; also : its bulb 2 : any of various plants of the same genus as the onion

24 Pieces

Color

Onions can be white, yellow, tan, or red. Choose a color that complements your background. I used a marbled white fabric for the onions. If the background shadows through, it may have to be lined. Line the onions in the same manner as the cauliflower (page 25). Five different green fabrics were used because, with so many leaves, it helps to define the individual leaf. A lavender fabric was used for the buds.

Appliqué Tips

Where you have a leaf turnover, you might find it easier to join the two pieces off the background and treat them as a unit to appliqué onto the background. These pieces include 1 and 2, 4, and 5, 9 and 10, 12 and 13, 14 and 15, and 16 and 17.

Finishing

Embroider the roots with two strands of black or brown floss using a stem stitch.

For needle-turn appliqué, add a ¼" turn-under allowance, then trim closer when appliquéing.

Peas

pea   1 a : a variable annual Eurasian vine *(Pisum sativum)* of the legume family that is cultivated especially for its rounded smooth or wrinkled edible protein-rich seeds b : the seed of the pea c plural : the immature pods of the pea with their included seeds

38 Pieces

Color

Three different green fabrics were used for the peas, pods, stems, and leaves. The peas should be light against the dark pod and the stems should be dark to contrast against leaf 1. Use two shades of pink for the buds.

Appliqué Tips

Make all the peas the same size. To make peas, cut a circle from an index card the size of the pea pattern. Cut out a fabric circle adding a ¼" seam allowance and run a basting stitch around the circle. Place the cardboard circle on the wrong side of the fabric and draw up the basting thread to gather. When the fabric is tight around the circle, press to keep the fabric in place. Remove the cardboard and place the peas on pod pieces 29 and 30. Slip stitch in place. Cover a portion of the peas with the remaining pods, 31 and 32.

Finishing

Embroider the pea vine with two strands of floss using a stem stitch.

For needle-turn appliqué, add a ¼" turn-under allowance, then trim closer when appliquéing.

For needle-turn appliqué, add a ¼" turn-under allowance, then trim closer when appliquéing.

Peppers

pep·per : CAPSICUM 1a; especially : a New World capsicum *(Capsicum annuum)* whose fruits are hot peppers or sweet peppers b : the hollow fruit of a pepper that is usually red or yellow when ripe

19 Pieces

Color

Three shades of green were used for the leaves and stems. A darker green was used for the inside of leaf 4. The buds are white. If your background is white, yellow or off-white fabric can be used. If your background shadows through, the buds may need to be lined. Use the same method as the cauliflower (page 25). You have many choices for your peppers – red, green, yellow, orange, or different shades of each. Be sure that pieces 1 and 17 are a deeper shade of the pepper color used.

Finishing

The veins in the leaves and peppers can be quilted during the final quilting of the pattern.

For needle-turn appliqué, add a ¼" turn-under allowance, then trim closer when appliquéing.

Squash

squash : any of various fruits of plants *(genus Cucurbita)* of the gourd family widely cultivated as vegetables; also : a plant and especially a vine that bears squashes

36 Pieces

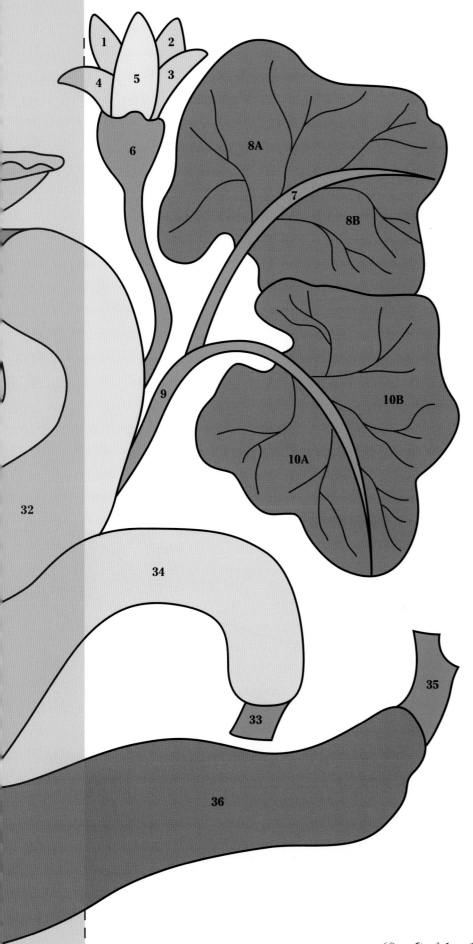

Color

Two shades of light and dark gold were used for the bud and flower. The squash can be gold, green, or yellow. Two light and dark green fabrics were used for the leaves.

Appliqué Tips

Appliqué the leaves and the leaf veins in the same manner as the beets (page 15). For the squash flower, baste 15, 18, 21, 24, and 27 in place on the background and appliqué the flower edges over this dark center using a lighter shade of gold.

Finishing

The smaller veins in the leaves can be quilted during the final quilting of the pattern.

For needle-turn appliqué, add a ¼" turn-under allowance, then trim closer when appliquéing.

For needle-turn appliqué, add a ¼" turn-under allowance, then trim closer when appliquéing.

Tomatoes

to·ma·to : 1 : the usually large rounded typically red or yellow pulpy berry of an herb (genus *Lycopersicon*) of the nightshade family native to South America 2 : a plant that produces tomatoes; especially : one (*Lycopersicon esculentum* syn. *L. lycopersicum*) that is a tender perennial widely cultivated as an annual for its edible fruit

22 Pieces

Color

Three different red fabrics were used for the tomatoes. One green fabric was used for the leaves and another green for the stems.

Appliqué Tips

On piece 13, leave one of the stems loose until stem 22 is appliquéd. Leave the tip of leaf 21 loose until stem 22 is in place. After 22 is appliquéd, sew the loose parts of 13 and 21.

Finishing

Leaf veins can be quilted during the final quilting of the pattern.

For needle-turn appliqué, add a ¼" turn-under allowance, then trim closer when appliquéing.

Veggie Quilts

VEGGIES FROM THE GOOD EARTH

Quilt size: 65" x 78"

Fabric requirements

Yardage is based on a 40" width.

Background and border................. 4¾ yards beige

Sashing, border, and binding.......... 1⅝ yards green

Veggies..scraps or fat quarters for
12 different veggies, with two
or more shades of each color

Leaves...scraps or fat quarters of at least
12 green fabrics

Border leaves, beans, and vines* ...scraps or fat quarters of 6 to 10
different green fabrics, ranging
from yellow-green to blue-green
and from light to dark

Border buds ....scraps of lavender or purple

* In planning your leaf colors, plan one section at a time using all of the green fabrics,
then move on to the next section. In this manner, you will have all the colors and
shades evenly dispersed around the border.

Appliqué the blocks

1. Prepare your fabrics as described on page 9. Keeping the grain straight, cut 12 squares 14" x 14" from the background fabric. These will be trimmed to size after the appliqué is finished.

2. Following the instructions on page 10, appliqué your choice of veggie patterns (pages 11–55) on the background squares. Embellish the veggies and leaves with embroidery if desired.

3. After the blocks are finished, wash out or remove any markings that still show. This should be done before pressing the blocks.

4. Press the finished block from the wrong side using a soft padded surface. This will keep the embroidery from becoming flat.

5. Cut away the background fabric under the larger appliqué pieces to eliminate any bulk and weight, making it easier to quilt.

6. After the appliqué is finished, it may be distorted. Spray with water to dampen and gently stretch. Pin the corners down on a padded surface to dry. Trim to 13½" square. This includes the seam allowance.

Assemble the quilt

1. Refer to the quilt assembly diagram and arrange the 12 blocks as desired in four rows of three blocks each.

2. Green strips were used to define the blocks, but they do not change the size of the blocks. To make the strips, cut eight green strips 1" x 13½". With wrong sides together, fold these strips in half lengthwise and press.

3. Sew these strips onto each side of the four center blocks with an ⅛" seam allowance (fig. 1). Sew the two outside blocks onto each of these center blocks with a ¼" seam allowance.

4. Cut three green strips 1" x 39½". With wrong sides together, fold these strips in half lengthwise and press. Sew these strips to the bottom of three of the rows with an ⅛" seam allowance. Sew the four rows together with a ¼" seam allowance.

5. For the inner border, cut five green strips 1½" across the fabric width and piece to produce two 52½" strips for the sides and two 41½"

Fig. 1. Sew the green strips to the four center blocks.

Quilt assembly

strips for the top and bottom. Sew the side borders to the assembled blocks first, then sew the top and bottom borders.

Construct the bean border

1. For the green bean border, cut two beige strips 12" x 56" for the sides and two beige strips 12" x 63" for the top and bottom. These borders will be trimmed to the correct size after the appliqué is finished. Prepare your fabric as you did with the blocks

2. The border pattern (pages 60–65) has been modified for ease of construction. Using the border pattern as a placement guide, start with the right side border and mark a free-flowing vine on the fabric. Use the border pattern leaves, beans, and peas to mark the remainder of the pattern. Bias tape can be used for the vines. Leave the extra side border fabric evenly divided on the top and bottom to trim off when the borders are ready to be attached.

3. Start the appliqué on the top of the right side border. Do not appliqué the leaves and stems on the ends of the side border until the top and bottom borders are in place. As you appliqué, you may need to leave openings in many of the stems and leaves to insert other stems. As these are inserted into openings, slip stitch the openings to secure the appliqué pieces.

4. When the right border is finished, reverse the pattern for the left side and appliqué in the same manner. Trim the side borders to 10½" x 54½" and sew them to the quilt.

5. The top and bottom border pattern guides are for one half of each border. Find the center of the top border. Mark the pattern as described in step 2 on the right side of the top border, making sure that the corner patterns match with the side border patterns. Reverse the pattern and mark the left side of the top border. Use the same method to mark the bottom border.

6. Appliqué the top and bottom borders, trim them to 10½" x 61½", and sew them to the quilt. Connect and appliqué the loose and hanging leaves, stems, and beans over the corner seams. Wash out any markings that show.

Top Right Border

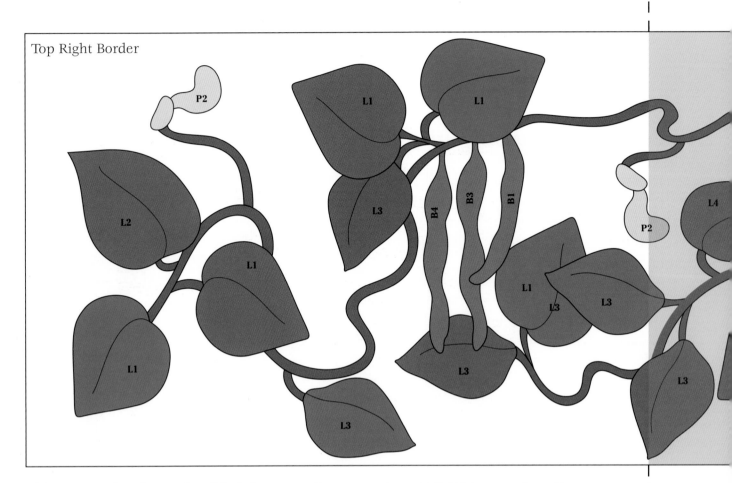

This pattern has been simplified for ease of construction. Add ¼" turn-under allowance, then trim closer when appliquing.

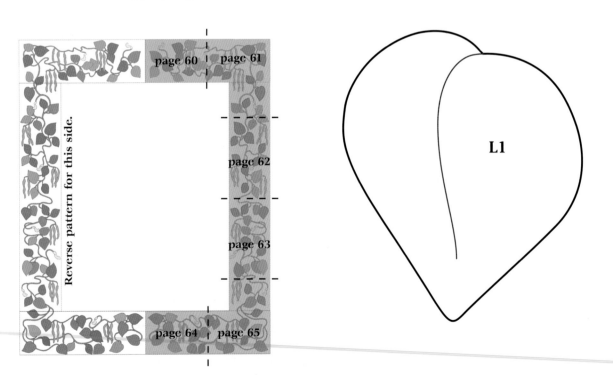

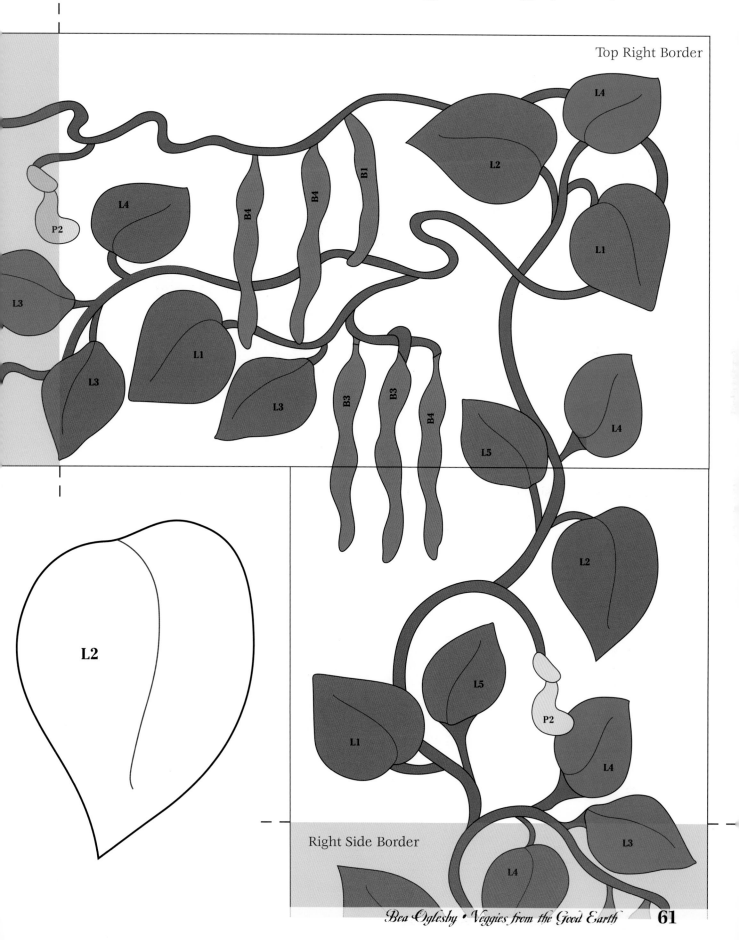

Top Right Border

Right Side Border

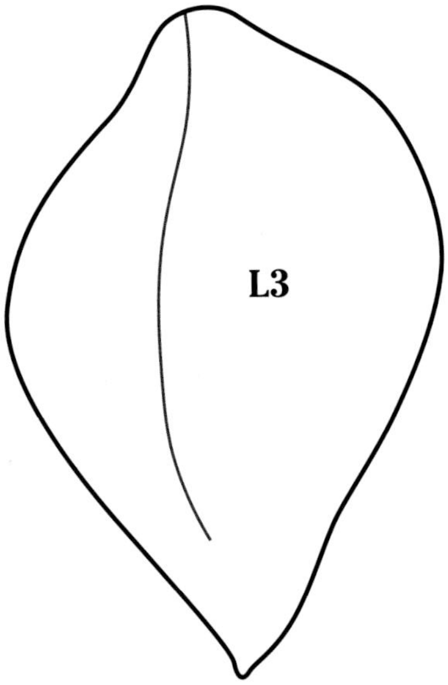

Right Side Border

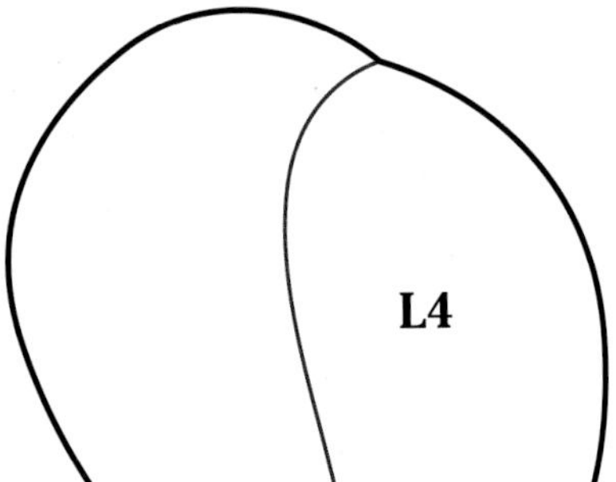

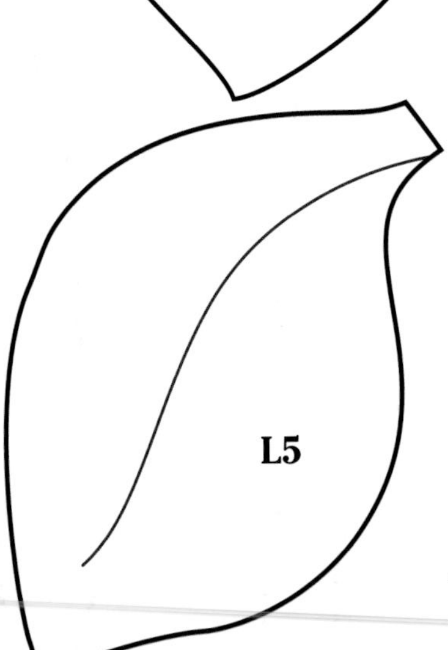

L3

L4

L5

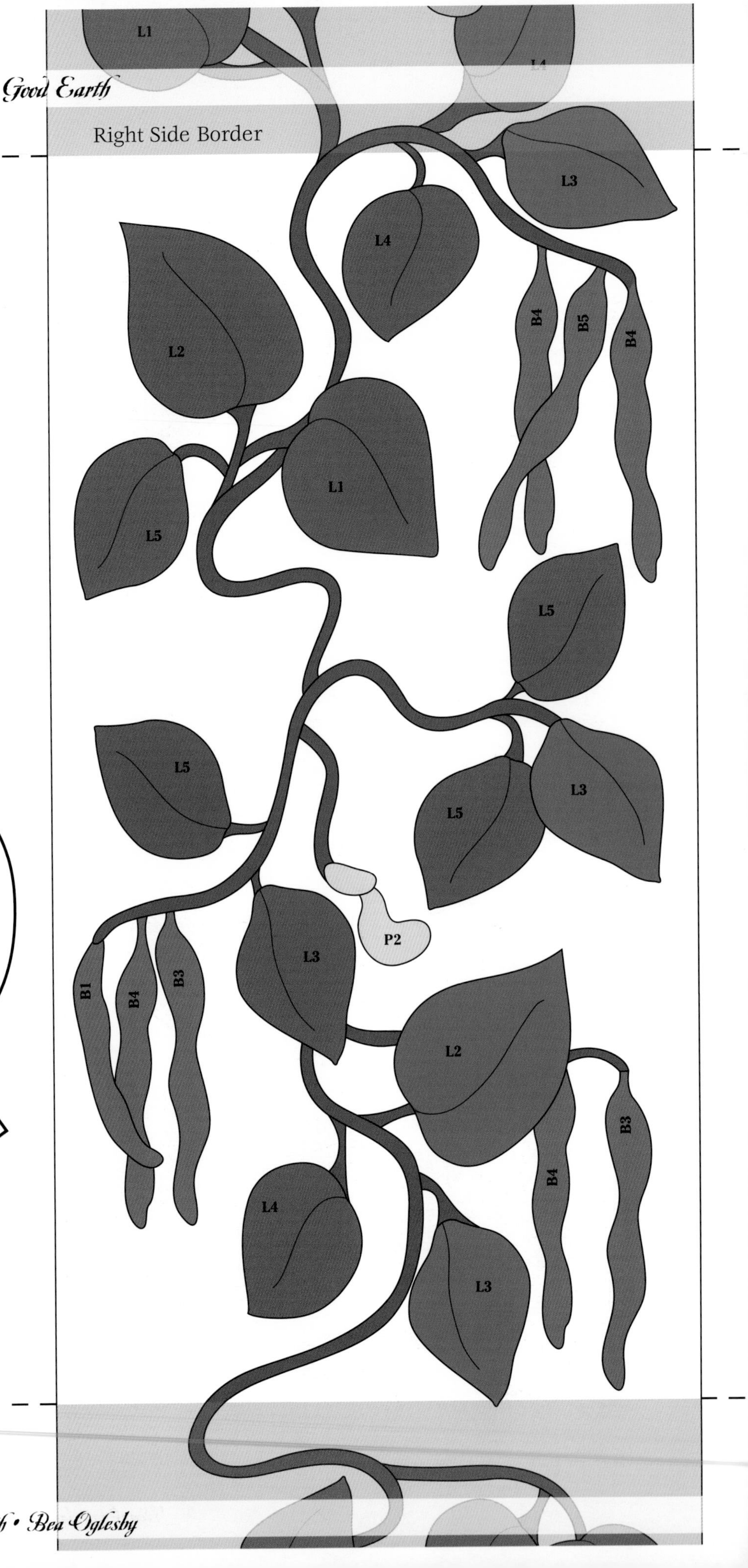

L1

L4

L3

L2

B4

B5

B4

L1

L5

L5

L5

L3

L5

P2

B1

B4

B3

L3

L2

B3

B4

L4

L3

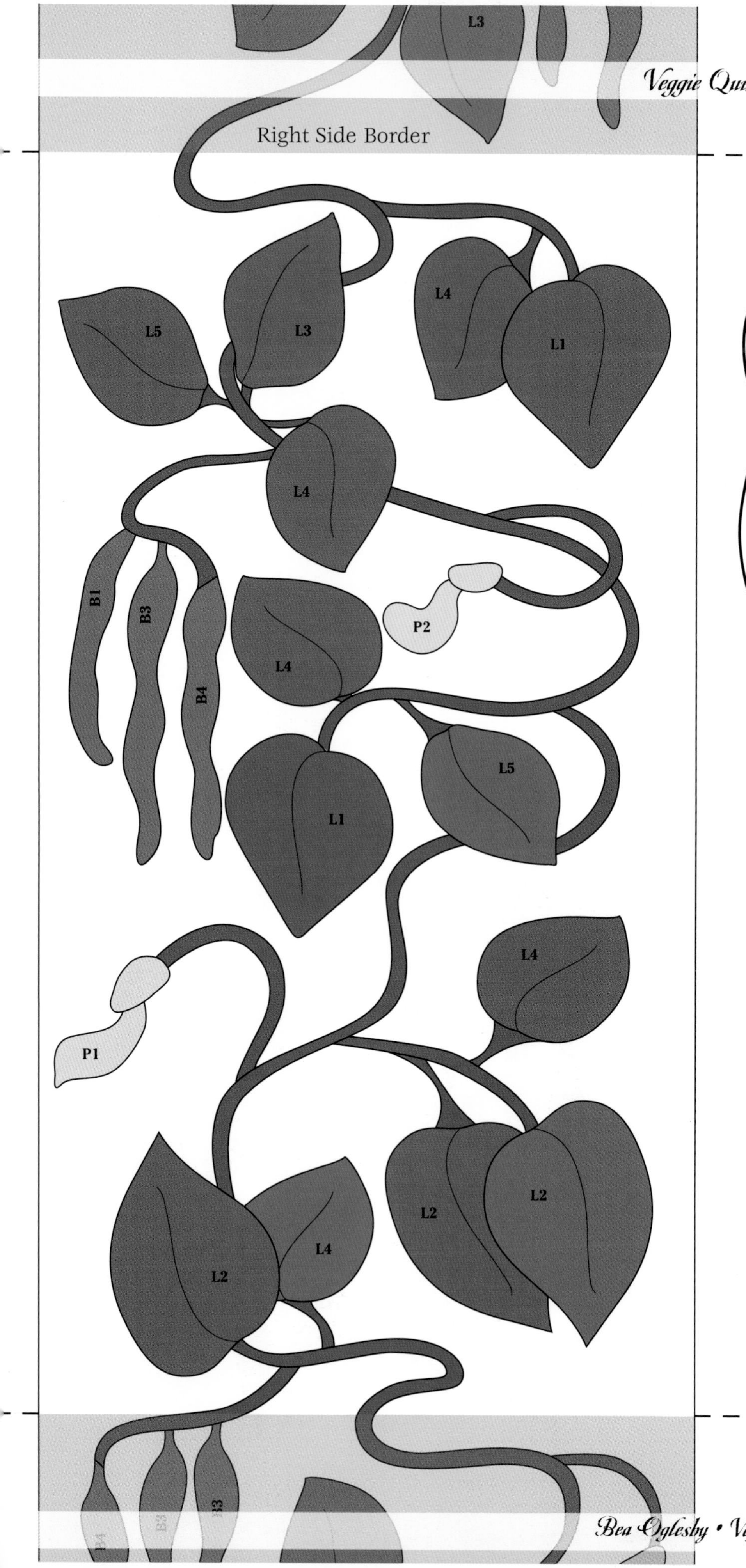
L3
Right Side Border
L5
L3
L4
L1
L4
B1
B3
B4
P2
L4
L1
L5
L4
P1
L2
L4
L2
L2
B3
B3
B4

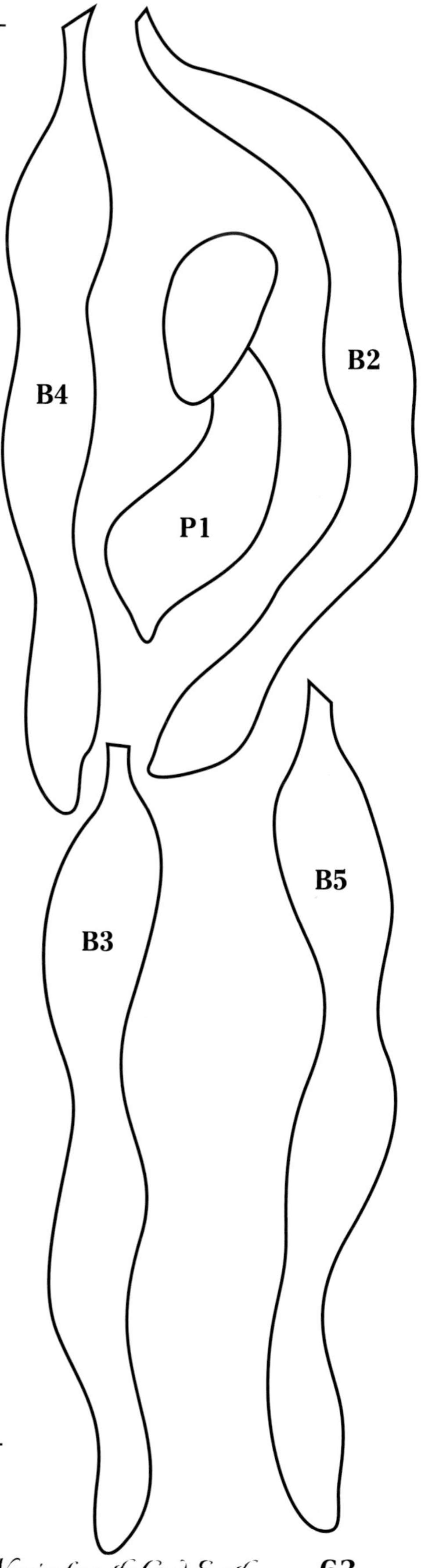
B4
B2
P1
B3
B5

Finish the quilt

1. For the outer border, cut seven green strips 2½" across the fabric width and piece to produce two 74½" strips for the sides and two 65½" strips for the top and bottom. Sew the side borders to the quilt top first, then sew the top and bottom borders.

2. Bind and quilt the layers. I quilted around each individual veggie, as well as the veins and designs in the leaves. The background was quilted in a geometric design.

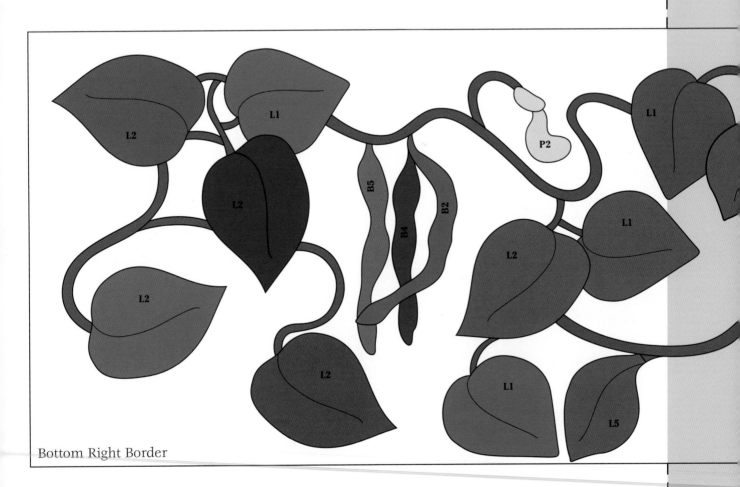

Bottom Right Border

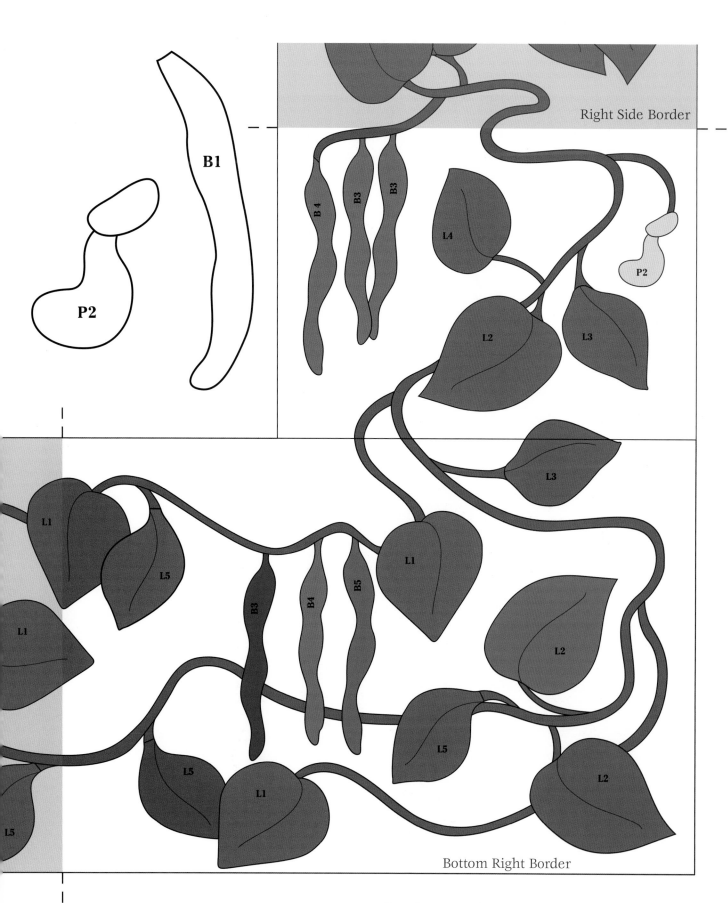

B1

P2

Right Side Border

B 4

B3

B3

L4

P2

L2

L3

L3

L1

L5

L1

B3

B4

B5

L1

L2

L1

L5

L5

L2

L5

L5

Bottom Right Border

VEGGIES IN A BASKET

Quilt size: 33" x 33"

Fabric requirements

Yardage is based on a 40" width.

Background .... 1 yard beige

Inner border..................................... ⅓ yard brown print

Outer border and binding.............. 1 yard black

Basket .... brown fat quarter

Veggies... scraps or fat quarters for the
different veggies and a minimum
of 12 different green fabrics

Although there are numerous pieces in this quilt, it is not difficult if you have planned your fabrics and colors, and each step is taken in sequence.

Appliqué options

Instructions for both traditional appliqué and fusible web appliqué are included. The color choices, arrangement, and sequence of the appliqué will be basically the same for either method.

Cut a 27" beige square for the background. This will be trimmed to size after the appliqué is finished.

Traditional appliqué

1. Following the instructions for appliqué (page 10) and the pattern instructions for the individual veggies, appliqué the veggie basket pattern (pages 70–75). It may be easier to work with only one veggie or one small section at a time rather than cutting out all 106 pieces at once. Note that 1A through 1J are parts inside the basket that are seen between the veggies.

2. Leave the top edge of the basket open until the veggies in the front have been appliquéd. After the blocks are finished, wash out or remove any markings that still show.

3. Cut away the background fabric under the larger appliqué pieces to eliminate any bulk and weight, making it easier to quilt. Press the finished block from the wrong side using a soft padded surface.

Fusible appliqué

1. Prepare the fabric the same as for traditional appliqué, but do not starch because it could interfere with the adherence of the fusible web. Mark the full-size pattern on the background fabric.

2. Follow the manufacturer's instructions and procedures for the fusible web. With fusible web, the patterns must be reversed to match the wallhanging. To reverse, copy the pattern from the back of the master pattern. It may be necessary to trace the back of the pattern with a marker to see it better.

3. Copy the reversed patterns on the smooth side of the fusible web and mark each piece with its number. Study the master pattern and the appliqué sequence carefully before you cut out the individual pieces.

4. Cut out each pattern piece and place this web template on the wrong side of the desired fabric. Fuse with an iron for only about 3 seconds. Cut out the pieces on the line, but be sure to add a seam allowance of ¼" in areas that will underlay another piece.

5. Peel off the paper backing and place the fusible side of the appliqué piece in its place on the marked background. Press with an iron approximately 20 seconds to melt the glue.

6. A narrow zigzag or a decorative sewing machine stitch on the edge of each piece gives the appliqué a finished look.

Finish the wallhanging

1. Trim the background block to 24½" square. This includes the seam allowance.

Quilt assembly

2. For the inner border, cut four brown print strips 2" x 26½". Sew these borders to the background and miter the corners. For the outer border, cut four black strips 3½" x 29½" and attach in the same manner as the inner border.

3. Bind and quilt the layers by hand or machine.

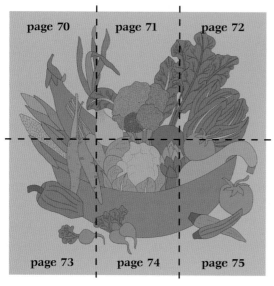

Basket pattern guide

For needle-turn appliqué, add a ¼" turn-under allowance, then trim closer when appliquing.

See page 73 for
pattern piece 1.

45B

44

45A

47A

47B

49A   49B   46

35B

48

52B

56A

52A   51

55

56B

54B

44

47B

58A

54A

46

58B

53

57

60A

50

62   59   60B

For needle-turn appliqué, add a ¼" turn-under allowance, then trim closer when appliquing.

For needle-turn appliqué, add a ¼" turn-under allowance, then trim closer when appliquing.

60A

62

59

60B

75

61

1I

78

79

1H

1J

83

82

88

84

1G

87

1

90

89

91

92

94

92

93

VEGGIE WALLHANGING

Quilt size: 55" x 55"

Fabric requirements

Yardage is based on a 40" width.

Background .... 3½ yards white

Basket, sashing, and binding .... 1 yard brown

Veggies .... scraps or fat quarters for the different veggies, with two or more shades of each color

Leaves .... minimum of 12 different light, medium, and dark green fabrics

Appliqué the blocks

1. Appliqué your choice of 12 veggies on 14" white background blocks as described in the VEGGIES FROM THE GOOD EARTH quilt (page 56). Trim the finished blocks to 13½". This includes the seam allowance.

2. Appliqué the Veggie Basket block on a 30" white square as described in the VEGGIES IN A BASKET wallhanging (page 66). Trim the finished block to 27½". This includes the seam allowance.

Assemble the quilt

1. Cut seven brown strips 2½" across the fabric width and set aside for the binding.

2. For the sashing, cut three brown strips 1½" across the fabric width and piece to produce two 55½" strips. Then, cut eight brown strips 1½" x 13½" and two brown strips 1½" x 27½".

3. Refer to the quilt assembly diagram to sew the veggie blocks, basket block, and sashing strips together.

Quilt assembly

4. Bind and quilt the layers by hand or machine.

About the Author

Combining sewing and drawing is a natural for Bea Oglesby. She considers gardens, flowers, and nature endless sources of ideas for appliqué. Although Bea did not start quilting until the mid-1980s, she has sewn most of her life having three daughters and a background in home economics. Bea has lived in Japan and has a certificate in Japanese flower arranging. She has also studied art, including charcoal sketching, oils, and watercolors.

Bea teaches and lectures in her community and belongs to several quilt guilds. She is also a volunteer in the community and at the Johnson County Library. She lives in Kansas with her husband. Other American Quilter's Society books by Bea include *Butterfly Album* (2004), *Birds and Flowers Album* (2003), and *Wildflower Album: Appliqué & Embroidery Patterns* (2000).

Other AQS Books

This is only a small selection of the books available from the American Quilter's Society. AQS books are known worldwide for timely topics, clear writing, beautiful color photos, and accurate illustrations and patterns. The following books are available from your local bookseller, quilt shop, or public library.

#7016   us$22.95

#7012   us$19.95

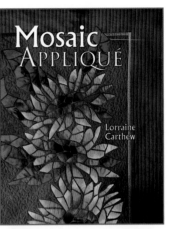

#7071   us$24.95

#7075   us$22.95

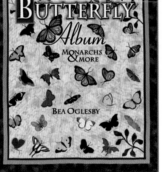

#6674   us$19.95

#7010   us$21.95

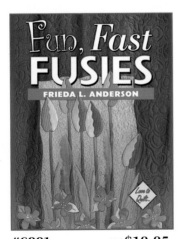

#6801   us$19.95

#6904   us$21.95

#6211   us$19.95

Look for these books nationally.
Call or **Visit** our Web site at

1-800-626-5420
www.AmericanQuilter.com